YO RSELF

Inspiration and advice
for body and soul...

PENELOPE
SACH

PENGUIN BOOKS

PENGUIN BOOKS

Published by the Penguin Group
Penguin Books Ltd, 27 Wrights Lane, London W8 5TZ, England
Penguin Putnam Inc., 375 Hudson Street, New York, New York 10014, USA
Penguin Books Australia Ltd, Ringwood, Victoria, Australia
Penguin Books Canada Ltd, 10 Alcorn Avenue, Toronto,
Ontario, Canada M4V 3B2
Penguin Books India (P) Ltd, 11 Community Centre,
Panchsheel Park, New Delhi – 110017, India
Penguin Books (NZ) Ltd, Cnr Rosedale and Airborne Roads,
Albany, Auckland, New Zealand
Penguin Books (South Africa) (Pty) Ltd, 5 Watkins Street,
Denver Ext 4, Johannesburg 2094, South Africa

Penguin Books Ltd, Registered Offices: Harmondsworth, Middlesex, England

First published in Australia by Penguin Books Australia Ltd 1996
Published in Penguin Books 1997
6 8 10 12 14 15 13 11 9 7 5
Copyright © Penelope Sach, 1996
All rights reserved
The moral right of the author has been asserted

Printed in England by William Clowes Ltd

A NOTE FROM THE AUTHOR

We're all susceptible to the effects of modern living, whether we're sports people, career professionals, homemakers or students; whether we're fifteen or fifty; whether we're male or female.

As a health consultant I see people with all manner of ailments every day. I develop nutritional programs for their individual needs and prescribe herbal and vitamin supplements where necessary. This book contains some insights from my work over the past ten years.

In many cases throughout this book I've made a general reference to the herbs and vitamins most useful for a particular condition. Use my suggestions as a guide, and consult a herbalist or naturopath to tailor the dose and application to your individual needs. Please note that any plant substance, whether used as food or medicine, externally or internally, can cause an allergic reaction in some people. Don't attempt self-treatment for serious or long-term problems or while you're undergoing a prescribed course of medical treatment without consulting a medical professional or qualified practitioner. And remember, always seek medical advice if symptoms persist.

*He lives long who enjoys life and who bears
no jealousy of others; whose heart harbours
no malice or anger; who sings a lot and cries
a little; who rises and retires with the sun;
who likes to work and knows how to rest.*

Shirali Mislimov,
Russian centenarian

TO START THE DAY

To cleanse the inner body before a
busy day, squeeze a quarter of a
fresh lemon in a glass of warm water
and add a teaspoon of honey.
It works wonders!

LITTLE BY LITTLE

Any large-scale accomplishment is
achieved only when tackled little by
little. Be patient and tackle only one
thing at a time. Then watch the big
picture unfold.

BREAKFAST ON THE RUN

For a delicious, quick and satisfying
breakfast, blend skim or soy milk
with a teaspoon each of lecithin
powder (helps the nerves) and
psyllium husks (contain fibre),
a mango or a banana, and a
teaspoon of honey.

A NATURAL RINSE FOR BLOND HAIR

Used regularly, a chamomile rinse
tones and adds life to dull, blond
hair, regardless of colour tints. Use
half a cup of organic chamomile
flowers to half a litre of boiled
water, let steep and strain. Rinse
your hair in the mixture and then
let it dry naturally.

LEARN TO LAUGH

Laughing helps relieve depression, pain and anxiety. It stimulates yet it relaxes, it gives every organ in the body a good work-out, and it's fun. Laughing has even been known to improve the condition of people suffering from high blood pressure. Learn to laugh heartily every day.

FEELING TIRED?

There are many causes of prolonged tiredness. Have a complete medical check-up concentrating on your iron levels, your liver and your immune system, and ask your naturopath for a suitable vitamin supplement for your lifestyle.

INCREASING YOUR SEX DRIVE

Getting adequate sleep, exercising in
fresh air and enjoying a balanced
diet will all help to increase your sex
drive, as will limiting your caffeine
and alcohol intake. But aside from
looking after your health, don't
forget to wear sexy clothes that
make you *want* to have sex.

CATCH UP WITH FRIENDS

When did you last spend quality time
with your friends? If the answer is
several weeks ago or, worse still, if
you can't remember, call up a friend
and arrange to spend some time
together. Don't let your friendships
slip into the background of your life,
no matter how busy you are.

WATCH YOUR CAFFEINE INTAKE

If you have around four cups of average-strength coffee or six cups of black tea a day, you may be caffeine-dependent. Limit your caffeine intake and avoid it completely if you have high blood pressure or if you suffer from anxiety or insomnia.

LAMENTING YOUR LANK HAIR?

If your hair is lank and brittle, include mineral- and silicon-rich foods in your diet. Such foods include oats, whole grains, yoghurt, almonds, alfalfa, onions, kelp, avocado, corn and sardines.

BROADEN YOUR HORIZONS

Read widely. Newspapers, journals
and magazines are all great reading
material if you find novels too heavy-
going. Reading is the best way to
broaden your knowledge and keep
yourself informed. And as any avid
reader will tell you – it's great fun.

BEFORE A WILD NIGHT OUT

Take a vitamin B or multi-vitamin supplement before a 'heavy' night out. Line your stomach by drinking a glass of milk or a cup of slippery elm tea, or by eating a banana. This slows down the absorption of alcohol into the bloodstream.

AFTER A WILD NIGHT OUT

If you've had a bit too much to drink, have two or three glasses of water or herbal tea when you get home. Take a vitamin C supplement that contains bioflavonoids, and have a hot shower. All this helps to flush out the overload of toxins in your body.

THE MORNING AFTER

To rid your body of that 'morning after' feeling, take a multi-vitamin supplement and eat a large, healthy breakfast with fresh juice or herbal tea. Have a swim or a sauna to 'sweat' out the acid build-up in your system. You'll feel terrific afterwards!

WHAT YOU EAT IS HOW YOU'LL FEEL

Be aware that what you eat today
will affect how you feel tomorrow.
Every time you choose to eat
healthy – or 'bad' – foods, you're
affecting the levels of energy and
vitality you have in reserve for
the next day.

ENJOY LIFE

When we push ourselves to enjoy life,
our food metabolises better, our
blood circulates more freely and
we have a greater drive to feel
and look great.

THE 'F' WORD

Fatigue is often a symptom of our struggle to keep up with the pace of modern living. Our adrenal glands become exhausted from lack of sleep, long hours and too much work. Ask your naturopath about herbs that assist the adrenal glands such as Gotu kola, Panax ginseng and Siberian ginseng.

SIMPLE SNACK IDEAS

If you're looking for quick, healthy snack ideas, consider a crunchy wholemeal or multigrain bread roll, fruit, a handful of nuts, rye and wholemeal biscuits, sushi, yoghurt, wholemeal scones or soup.

RESTORING MOISTURE

If your skin lacks moisture, include
unsaturated fats – such as cold-
pressed olive oil, flaxseed oil,
sunflower oil and fish oils – in your
diet. Or you may prefer to take one
or two capsules of salmon oil a day.

A WORD ON LONG LIFE

Li Chung Yun lived to be 156 years old and when asked to what he attributed his long life he answered: 'inward calm, unprocessed foods, moderate eating and plenty of exercise'. Think about it.

TIPS FOR YOUR FINGERTIPS

Don't despair about cracked and
damaged nails. Try including grains
(such as brown rice), more fresh
vegetables and yoghurt in your diet.
Rub almond or avocado oil into your
cuticles each night, and take a
calcium–magnesium supplement
daily until the problem
is resolved.

90% HEALTHY, 10% NAUGHTY

Give yourself a break and allow yourself one naughty treat a day. A cup of delicious Italian coffee (not too strong) or a small sweet is a fitting reward for being good *most* of the time.

MEDITATION – FITNESS FOR YOUR MIND

Meditation isn't passive relaxation: it's an exercise program for your mind. It can bring you increased creativity, calmness, energy, understanding and spiritual fulfilment. Learn the techniques of meditation and practise daily.

RINSE AWAY YOUR DANDRUFF

Thyme has mild antiseptic properties that can help clear dandruff. Add four teaspoons of dried thyme to two cups of water, boil and strain. When cool, rinse your hair in the solution and leave to dry.

THE GIFT OF WATER

Water nourishes our blood and our
cells, and prevents the build-up of
toxic wastes in our bodies. We can't
survive without it. Make a conscious
effort to drink water or herbal tea
daily, around six to eight glasses.
Record your habits for a week,
as sometimes we can forget to
drink at all!

FLYING COMFORTABLY

If you're prone to bloating when on
an aeroplane, eat yoghurt daily and
avoid yeasty foods a week before
your trip. Order a vegetarian dish
on the plane, avoid alcohol and
drink water.

IMPOTENCE — A LACK OF ZINC?

Impotence is often caused by a lack of zinc. Include zinc-rich foods such as oysters, eggs, onions and pumpkin seeds in your diet, and try saw palmetto, ginseng and Gotu kola herbs. Stop smoking and avoid alcohol.

TAKE A BREAK

When you feel tired and run down,
take some time out and have a
holiday. It sounds simple enough, yet
so many people just don't listen to
their bodies. Taking a holiday – even
a very short one – is the perfect way
to energise your mind and body.

'OH, MY ACHING FEET!'

Soothe aching feet by soaking them
in a hot foot bath with a tablespoon
of Epsom salts and three drops of
peppermint oil. Massage your feet,
concentrating on the arches.
Afterwards, stretch your feet and
toes by moving up and down on
the balls of your feet for
a few minutes.

TIPS FOR NIGHT OWLS

If you work through the night, try drinking liquorice tea: it will give you a boost of energy. Snack on foods that are high in energy, such as a boiled egg, chicken patties, hot soups, dried fruit and nuts.

TAKE TEN DEEP BREATHS

When you feel yourself becoming
entangled in a problem you can't
solve, take ten deep breaths and put
the problem aside. Deep breathing
increases the flow of oxygen to your
brain and slows your heart rate.
Later, consider a way to solve the
problem – *differently*.

THE BENEFITS OF SAGE TEA

One or two cups of sage tea a day
will help to heighten your spirits and
alleviate depression. As it assists in
the balancing of oestrogen levels,
it's particularly useful for
menopausal women.

DOZING AT THE OFFICE?

Keep a bottle of peppermint or rosemary oil on your desk and rub a few drops into your temples if you often find yourself becoming sleepy. One tiny drop rubbed near your nostrils will also awaken you quickly (and could avoid a potentially embarrassing situation!).

KEEPING TRACK OF TIME

If your days seem to be passing you
by, keep track of them by keeping a
journal. Explore your creativity as
you explore your day.

FOR WOMEN ON THE PILL

The contraceptive pill can drain your
body of essential vitamins, so it's
advisable to take one multi-vitamin
supplement a day. If you've gained
weight on the pill, avoid fats and
yeasty foods such as bread, wine
and cheese.

JUST SAY 'NO'

There's nothing wrong with saying
'No'. In fact, saying 'No' every once
in a while is a matter of survival.
Learn to delegate if you have too
many commitments or if you're just
too tired. And don't feel guilty
about it!

TAKING THE STING
OUT OF RASHES

Taking a fish oil capsule (such as salmon oil or cod liver oil) once a day and including more fresh fish in your diet can help prevent beard and shaving rashes. Vitamin E, paw paw or calendula cream will also help.

ACNE RELIEF

To help relieve this persistent
condition, drink dandelion root tea
two or three times a day to flush out
toxins from your liver. Cut out fatty
foods from your diet and avoid
alcohol, coffee and tea. One
echinacea tablet a day can
also be useful.

GOOD HEALTH FOR
A GOOD HOLIDAY

Prior to that well-deserved and long-
awaited holiday, try to detoxify your
system by not overeating, keeping
your alcohol intake to a minimum
and including lots of fresh vegetables
and juices in your daily diet. Then go
ahead and enjoy yourself.

CAN'T SLEEP?

If you're having trouble sleeping,
avoid caffeine and try drinking a tea
(or taking a tablet) made from
passionflower and vervain. Taking
a calcium supplement or a valerian
tablet just before you go to bed
may also help.

BE REALISTIC

If you've made the decision to
increase the amount of physical
activity in your life, be realistic.
Initially try to exercise three times a
week for fifteen minutes. Then slowly
increase this when you're ready.

LIGHT MEALS FOR
LATE NIGHTS

Even if you get home late, make sure
you have something small to eat,
especially if you've been drinking.
Eat light foods such as a sandwich,
steamed vegetables, a bowl of soup, a
salad or a plate of boiled pasta with
olive oil and a touch of herb salt.

HAVE A MASSAGE

You wouldn't hesitate to see a doctor
when you're sick, so don't hesitate to
see a masseur or masseuse when your
muscles are tight and painful. You'll
feel calm and restored.

BEFORE A SPORTING HOLIDAY ...

Try to exercise regularly at least six
weeks before you embark on that
skiing trip or that surfing holiday.
You'll help to avoid injury and
improve your fitness level.

BALDING?

Increase the circulation to your scalp
by exercising, eating spicy foods and
taking a herb called Ginkgo biloba.
Try rubbing a few drops of rosemary
oil into your scalp daily, and work
at keeping your stress levels
under control.

An instant 'lift'

Keep a vase of fresh flowers in
a place where you can see them
throughout the day. They'll give the
room – and you – an instant 'lift'.

RELIEF FROM TENSION HEADACHES

Dilute two or three drops of lavender oil in a teaspoon of sweet almond oil. Breathing deeply, massage your temples and neck. Keep an eye out for capsules or tablets of relaxing herbs such as chamomile, lemon balm, linden flowers or valerian.

DEALING WITH ARTHRITIS

Drink a glass of fresh celery juice
every day, and minimise your intake
of acidic foods such as citrus fruit,
cheese, wine and sugar. Take a fish
oil capsule – preferably before you
go to bed – to lubricate
your joints.

A TIP FOR
NURSING MOTHERS

Alfalfa tea or tablets are high in
minerals and are excellent both for
improving the quality of your milk
and for helping to overcome poor
lactation. It's good for you and for
your baby.

BAGS UNDER YOUR EYES?

Bags under the eyes may be associated with fluid retention. Have your kidneys checked and find out whether you have any hereditary cardiovascular problems. Hormonal imbalances and food allergies may be other factors to consider.

IT'S *YOUR* RESPONSIBILITY

Remember: you aren't responsible for
the misfortunes in your life, but you
are responsible for doing something
about them.

WHEN YOUR WHITES ARE OFF-WHITE

Yellowish eyes are often caused by a sluggish liver. Cut out all fatty foods and alcohol for two months. Drink dandelion root tea, and include artichoke, endive, watercress, raw apples and raw pears in your diet.

IT'S *THAT* TIME OF THE MONTH

If you suffer from tender breasts and
painful cramps during your period,
try taking vitamin B6 and a
magnesium tablet every day a week
before your period is due.

THINK YOUNG

If you feel old, you're probably thinking old. Think young, surround yourself with young people, engage in activities you enjoy, and rekindle a true love of life. Life is not a dress rehearsal: it's the real thing!

TO RELIEVE A STIFF NECK

Relax in a hot bath containing half a
cup of Epsom salts and four or five
drops of lavender oil. Massage your
shoulder and neck muscles and
breathe deeply. Afterwards, apply
heat to the area with either a
menthol cream or a hot
face washer.

SETTLING A
NERVY STOMACH

If you suffer from the discomfort of
a nervy or acidic stomach, mix a
teaspoon of slippery elm powder into
half a glass of warm water or milk
and drink it before each meal. Avoid
white wine, cheese, tomatoes, vinegar
and refined sugar products.

STRENGTHEN YOUR BONES

To strengthen your bones and avoid
the onset of osteoporosis, eat
mineral-rich foods such as yoghurt,
low-fat cheese and milk, oats, barley
and buckwheat. You may also need
a calcium supplement if you're
menopausal or allergic to
dairy products.

TO SOOTHE SUNBURN

Immediately squeeze a vitamin E capsule (or several, depending on the extent of the burn) over the affected area. Aloe vera gel is also very helpful in relieving the discomfort of this and other burns.

CRAVING ALCOHOL?

Eat small amounts of food
throughout the day to give you a
'lift', and substitute one glass of
alcohol with a glass of freshly
squeezed juice. Snack on pure
liquorice candy, a piece of fruit
or a muesli bar.

REFINE YOUR
RESPONSE TO STRESS

Stress affects everyone equally; it's
the response to stress that differs
from person to person. Focus on your
reaction to stress, not on the stress
itself. Being able to deal with stress
in a dignified, effective manner helps
build character and heightens
self-esteem.

FIGHTING THE COMMON COLD

If you have a fever, abstain from solid foods and drink fresh fruit and vegetable juices, peppermint tea or water. A cup of hot water with a squeeze of lemon juice and a teaspoon of honey drunk regularly will help to clear mucus. Vitamin C supplements may also help.

PREVENTING
PEPTIC ULCERS

When drunk daily, papaya juice is
wonderful in helping to prevent
peptic ulcers, as is a regular intake
of carrot and raw cabbage juice, and
aloe vera juice. Avoid citrus juices,
tomatoes and vinegar, and try to
keep your stress levels
to a minimum.

GO EASY ON YOURSELF

If you're tired, upset or stressed,
don't force yourself to eat. Drink a
nourishing soup or juice, which is
gentle on your digestive system.
When the stress has passed, eat a
hearty, nutritious meal.

TAKE A CLOSER LOOK
AT YOUR SKIN

If you have what appear to be small
pimples under your skin, make sure
you're emptying your bowel
completely. Adding bran or psyllium
husks to a nutritious cereal will help
you to do this. You could also
include garlic in your diet to help
kill unwanted bacteria.

FULFIL YOUR DREAMS

Unfulfilled dreams can contribute to
unhappiness, resentment and
depression, particularly later in life.
Life is too short – follow
your dreams.

FRESHEN YOUR BREATH

Bad breath can be caused by a
number of factors: undigested food
and constipation, or even tooth and
gum decay, tonsillitis and sinusitis.
Visit your doctor and your dentist
and explore these possible causes.

A WORD ON
HARMFUL EMISSIONS

Leaded emissions from cars, planes,
and industrial sources are one of the
harmful side effects of modern living.
Symptoms of lead poisoning include
loss of appetite, fatigue, sudden
weight loss and nervousness. Early
detection from your doctor is
important, so be vigilant with
your health.

ITCHY EARS?

Itchy ears are often caused by a mild
fungus. Keep your ears dry and cut
down on your yeast and sugar intake.
A drop of tea tree oil on a cotton
bud applied *only* to the *outside*
of your ear can help to relieve some
of the itching.

POOR DIET, POOR MEMORY

A poor diet, too much refined sugar and irregular eating habits aggravate the sugar levels in the blood, and can lead to forgetfulness. Eat small, regular, healthy snacks in between three balanced daily meals, and try taking the herb Gingko biloba, which promotes circulation to the brain.

AFTER YOU'VE QUIT

When you've made the decision to
give up smoking, do your body
another favour by cleansing it with
loads of water and fresh juices.
Vitamin B and C supplements will
also help. Oat porridge and
chamomile tea are excellent for
calming the nerves.

FOR SORE, STINGING EYES

If your eyes are sore, lie down and
place a warm wet chamomile tea bag
over your eyes for five to ten
minutes. It will help you to relax and
avoids a dependency on eye drops.
This treatment is also good
for children.

REVERSE YOUR ROUTINE

We can unconsciously become slaves
to routine, doing the same old things
in the same old way, each and every
day. Change your habits every so
often: prepare an exotic dinner
instead of the usual weekly dish, read
a novel instead of the newspaper, or
go for a walk if you usually ride a
bike. You'll feel refreshed.

A HOMEMADE REMEDY
FOR CYSTITIS

If you're prone to cystitis, drink
homemade barley water. Mix half a
cup of pearl barley with one litre of
water and simmer for twenty minutes.
Strain and add honey to taste.

SHORT OF BREATH?

If you're feeling stressed after a big day and you're a little short of breath, lie on a rolled towel placed longways across the middle of your back. Breathe deeply and slowly for five minutes, and feel your breathing return to normal.

SOLAR ENERGY

On sunny days, try to spend a couple
of minutes outdoors to catch a few
rays of sunlight. Sunlight gives you a
boost of vitamin D and makes you
feel alive. (Always wear a sunscreen,
of course!)

LOOK GOOD, FEEL GOOD

Don't save all those wonderful clothes, shoes or jewellery for so-called 'special' occasions. Every day is special! Wear whatever makes you feel fabulous – *every* day.

EYE FITNESS

Keep your eyes healthy by drinking
carrot juice regularly. Have your eyes
checked annually and buy the best
lenses available should you need
them. Consider eye exercises, which
can be very effective.

A HINT FOR YOUR HEELS

If your heels are cracked and dry,
soak your feet in warm water for five
minutes and then buff your heels
with a rough natural sea sponge. Dry
your feet thoroughly, and moisturise
with vitamin E and jojoba cream.
You'll need to do this regularly
for the best results.

ONE ORANGE, ONE WHITE, ONE GREEN

Try to eat three vegetables – one orange, one white, one green – every day. Each has different vitamins and minerals that your body needs. Ideally you should aim to eat half your intake of vegetables raw.

TO WHITEN
YOUR TEETH ...

Moisten your toothbrush with water
and then dip it into some baking
soda. Brush your teeth with this
paste once a week to help whiten and
brighten them. Then smile!

SPRING-CLEAN YOUR MIND

Try spring-cleaning your house,
office, drawers, wardrobes, and
cupboards. You'll find that the
process of sorting and cleaning,
disposing and retaining, is as much
a mental spring-clean as a
physical one.

DON'T FORGET TO CHEW!

Taking the time to chew your food
thoroughly will assist digestion, and
actually help you eat less. The old
Chinese healers believed that chewing
is the key to better health, as it
takes the load off the stomach's
digestive enzymes.

S-T-R-E-T-C-H

To achieve all-over body tone and help prevent injury before exercise, make it a ritual to stretch for ten minutes – morning and night. You'll find it gives you a greater sense of wellbeing, too.

A SWEET REPLACEMENT

Try using honey instead of refined
sugar in your tea, coffee and
cooking. Refined sugar robs your
body of nutritive elements and can
contribute to disease and tooth
decay. Honey is much better for
you, and it tastes delicious.

HENNA – A HELP FOR YOUR HAIR

Hair can often fall out as a result of too much colouring. If you're losing hair in this way, try using henna hair colours. They come from the natural dye of the henna plant so they won't damage your hair. In fact, they can positively transform dull and lifeless hair.

AN OLD-FASHIONED PICK-ME-UP

If you want to avoid taking vitamin
supplements but you need a pick-me-
up, try old-fashioned brewer's yeast.
Use one teaspoon in a glass of water
or milk daily. Full of vitamin B,
brewer's yeast also assists
digestion, and is particularly
useful for the delicate digestive
tracts of the elderly.

A CURE FOR CONSTIPATION

Drinking one or two cups of senna
tea a day is terrific in helping to
alleviate constipation, as is a
teaspoon of psyllium husks once or
twice a day on cereal or in a glass of
water. Avoid large amounts of animal
protein and think about the ways in
which you could eliminate stress and
nervousness from your life.

THE HUMBLE EGG

Don't forget the protein-rich
egg – boiled, poached or scrambled.
Leave out the yolk if you have
high cholesterol. (An omelette made
from eggwhites is delicious.)

JUST ONE GLASS
OF RED WINE

Research has shown that red wine
contains anti-oxidant properties that
help prevent cardiovascular diseases.
But, as always, moderation is the
key. Enjoy just one glass of
red wine a day.

A WORD ON MENOPAUSE

During menopause, the level of
oestrogen in a woman's body begins
to decrease. To help alleviate the
unpleasant symptoms of menopause
it's important to eat foods containing
plant oestrogen such as soy products,
alfalfa, bean shoots, parsley,
basil and sage.

WATER – THE 'GOOD' DRINK

For every cup of coffee, tea or alcohol you drink, have a glass of water. Water helps guard against dehydration and will flush out the toxins remaining in your system from the 'not-so-good' drinks.

'CLEANING' YOUR BLOOD

A glass of carrot and raw beetroot juice drunk regularly will help to 'clean' your blood. Beetroot contains vitamins A, B and C and loads of minerals. It's excellent for your liver, kidneys, spleen and gall bladder.

A REMEDY FOR CRACKING JOINTS

If you have cracking joints, try
mixing one teaspoon of apple cider
vinegar in a glass of warm water.
Taken daily it's a great help for
those with gout, rheumatism
and gravel.

SELF-MASSAGE FOR STRESS RELIEF

The upper shoulders and neck are notorious for storing stress. Firmly massage a sore neck and shoulders with a mixture of hot olive oil and two to three drops of pine oil every night for instant relief.

SOOTHING DRY
'WINTER' SKIN

With less humidity in the air during
the cold winter months, skin can
become dry and papery. If your skin
becomes dry in winter, mix sorbolene
cream with some jojoba oil.
It's cheap and very effective.

A CURIOUS CURE
FOR COUGHS

To soothe a sore throat and relieve
you of a cough, pour one tablespoon
of honey over a raw onion cut in
quarters. Place in a small dish and
bake in an oven for twenty minutes.
While still warm, sip the honey syrup
from the onion. It's an effective
remedy for the whole family.

BECOME A TOURIST

Imagine you're a tourist and explore your city the way a tourist would. Book yourself into a hotel, visit art galleries and museums, join a city bus tour, walk streets you wouldn't normally enter and eat in new restaurants. There's a lot of tourist information available to help you find new and interesting things to do.

SWITCH TO
VEGETABLE SALT

Try using vegetable salt instead of
table salt as a condiment. Vegetable
salt is made from dried vegetables,
which contain a balance of
potassium, magnesium and calcium.
It's better for you and, unlike table
salt (which is sodium chloride), it
won't make you retain fluid.

RESTLESS SLEEP?

If you're sleeping poorly and lightly,
remove all preservatives, additives
and stimulants from your diet –
including caffeine, spices and
alcohol – and avoid eating
a large dinner.

REPEAT AFTER ME ...

During a stressful time it can help
to take a deep breath and say to
yourself over and over: 'I'm feeling
relaxed and in control'. It really
works if you practise it regularly.

FOR SMOOTH, SEXY LIPS

Make your own lip balm by combining one tablespoon of melted beeswax with one tablespoon of olive or sweet almond oil. You may add a few drops of lavender or rose oil if you wish. Pour the mixture into a very small jar and apply to your lips two or three times a day.

TO STRENGTHEN
WEAK HAIR

You can improve the texture of weak,
thin hair by drinking two cups of
rosemary, alfalfa and sage tea
every day. Taken in this way,
the brew will gradually help to
strengthen your hair.

ITCHING RELIEF

Before you start rubbing all manner
of creams into your skin, try taking
an evening primrose oil capsule with
two or three cups of the purest
dandelion root tea daily. Eliminate
fats from your diet where possible,
and avoid drinking wine and
orange juice.

A MORNING TEA
PICK-ME-UP

Try eating a mango and fresh yoghurt
for morning tea. Mangoes are a
filling and nutritious energy booster,
while yoghurt contains a bacteria
called acidophilus, which helps to
digest food.

JUST ONE GOOD DEED

Turn your thoughts away from your
present situation and think about the
ways in which you could help those
around you. Try doing even just one
good deed a day. You'll help to
promote universal happiness –
including your own.

A SOLUTION TO SPLIT ENDS

Unsightly split ends are a common source of frustration. Have a good haircut and ask your hairdresser for a moisturising oil to apply to the tips of your hair. Take a fish oil capsule every day, and increase your daily intake of calcium, magnesium and zinc.

TO AID DIGESTION

Eat more natural digestives such as
limes, lemons, onions, garlic, chilli,
paprika, papaya and pineapple if
your digestion is poor. Eating slowly
and eating smaller meals more
frequently will also help.

WAXING WOES

Ingrown hairs from waxing and shaving are a real nuisance and can often be very painful. Echinacea cleans the blood and assists the functioning of the sebaceous glands, and is excellent for treating ingrown hairs. Take one or two echinacea tablets a day until the condition improves.

THE SOUND OF SILENCE

For a few minutes every day, close
your eyes and listen to the sound of
silence. It's so often the most
beautiful 'music' of all.

HAYFEVER RELIEF

If you suffer from the irritation
of hayfever, take two or three
bioflavonoid tablets with two or
three cups of eyebright and
peppermint tea each day. You'll
breathe a sigh of relief.

PMS

Take two or three evening primrose oil capsules daily about ten days before premenstrual symptoms usually surface. To relieve nervous tension during this time, drink relaxing teas such as chamomile tea and vervain tea.

LEARN FROM YOUR DREAMS

Dreams reveal a lot about what our true needs are. Keep a dream diary and write about your dreams: the characters, events, emotions, symbols – even your feelings as you wake up. Analyse your dreams (there are many books on the subject to help you), and think about what your dreams may be telling you.

ALL-OVER SKIN BEAUTY

Invest in a brush with natural
bristles. Starting at the soles of your
feet, brush your limbs in long,
upward strokes, concentrating on dry
areas such as elbows and heels. Use a
gentle, circular motion for your
torso. With regular brushing, your
skin will look polished and healthy.

ALL ABOUT
SUNFLOWER SEEDS

High in vitamins B and E, sunflower
seeds make a tasty snack. Sprinkle
sunflower seeds over your cereal, mix
them with other nuts or eat them
raw. Chewing sunflower seeds can
also be helpful for people trying to
quit smoking.

A TEA FOR NAUSEA RELIEF

A cup of peppermint tea with a pinch
of fresh or powdered ginger relaxes
the gall bladder and calms the
digestive enzymes. It brings fast
relief from nausea.

YOGA AND YOU

The word 'yoga' means union, and
the practice of yoga strives to effect
a union between the body and the
mind, the mind and the soul. Regular
practice helps to strengthen and tone
the muscles, and it's a great way to
learn to breathe deeply and relax.
Try it.

A SIMPLE WEIGHT-LOSS TIP

Don't eat until you feel as though you'll burst. Eat slowly, and stop eating when you're two-thirds full.

NOTES ON NIGHTMARES

While nightmares can be caused by a trauma of some kind, they are often simply the result of overeating. Large amounts of stimulants (such as caffeine and alcohol) in your diet, and overheating during sleep, also contribute to sleep disturbances.

TREATING COLD SORES

Unfortunately, once you've developed a cold sore, the condition is likely to recur when your immune system is under stress. When a cold sore does develop, obtain a lemon balm tincture from a herbalist and dab it on the infection.

DRINK, DRINK, DRINK

If you need encouragement to drink
more water, buy a colourful carafe,
jug or bottle and a glass, and keep
them filled with sparkling fresh water
in a place where you can see them.
You'll just *want* to drink!

THE EYES HAVE IT

Dust, computer screens, bright lights
and pollution – it's no wonder our
eyes can become red and sore, and
our sight a little blurry. Try
splashing cold water on your eyes
every morning to help keep them
working well, and include more
orange vegetables in your diet.

SOOTHING SOUNDS

Have a listen to one of the many CDs
and audio tapes available featuring
tranquil, natural sounds. They're
perfect for meditation
and relaxation.

SUGGESTIONS FOR
SINUS RELIEF

Echinacea (with vitamin C) capsules
are very effective in bringing about
relief from blocked sinuses. Inhaling
peppermint oil is also terrific: use
two or three drops of peppermint oil
on a tissue or in an oil burner.

A 'RED WINE' TEA

For that red wine taste without the
alcohol, drink hawthorn berry tea. It
has anti-oxidant properties that
improve circulation.

FIGHTING FAT

Remember: to lose fat, don't eat fat.
It's as simple as that.

SWOLLEN ANKLES?

Poor circulation and fluid retention
are often the culprits behind swollen
ankles. Have a medical check-up, and
try soaking your feet for ten to
fifteen minutes in a hot foot bath
with a tablespoon of Epsom salts.

CHECK-UPS FOR FEMALE TWENTY-SOMETHINGS

There are a number of health checks essential for every woman in her twenties. As well as general health (including a blood pressure test), gynaecological, dental and eye check-ups, women should also perform their own breast and skin cancer examinations.

ACQUIRE NEW SKILLS

Whatever your career or your
lifestyle, there are always
opportunities for reskilling and
improvement. Find out about short
courses that interest and challenge
you, and enjoy the professional and
personal benefits.

FEELING THE STRAIN?

When your eyes feel tired and sore,
and your sight becomes a little
blurry, stop what you're doing.
Gently press on your eyelids with the
palms of your hands, then rest your
eyes for a few minutes. Try to take
regular breaks from whatever you're
doing to avoid eye strain.

A GREEN IDEA

Buy a few good-quality plants and take pleasure in looking after them – and talking to them! Many people find 'indoor gardening' very relaxing, and the plants certainly liven up the home or office. Plants also purify the air you breathe, absorbing carbon dioxide and releasing oxygen.

THE LAW OF KARMA

Always be aware of the choices you
make and of their consequences.
The law of karma states that the
consequences of our decisions
return to us in some way.
Generate happiness and success,
and they will return to you
as the fruits of karma.

BOOST YOUR
IMMUNE SYSTEM

To help prevent minor ailments from
developing in the cold winter months,
take an echinacea tablet every day.
In addition to this, include lots
of garlic (preferably raw), onions,
fruit and green vegetables in your diet
to help keep your immune system
in top shape.

ENJOY *FRESH* AIR

Pollution is an unfortunate by-product of city living. Make time for a brisk walk in a nearby park, on a beach or on a walking track where you can rely on a dose of fresh air away from busy roads. Take a deep breath and feel the difference.

FIGHTING CELLULITE

Yes, you *can* do something about cellulite. Try sipping the juice of a lemon once a day to help your liver and gall bladder digest fats, and eat plenty of fresh fruit and vegetables. Daily dry brushing and massaging, along with regular exercise and lots of water, will help your body fight cellulite.

YOU MAY HAVE A FOOD ALLERGY

Have you ever felt extremely tired after eating a meal? If you have, you may be allergic to a particular food group. Your doctor can perform a number of simple allergy tests, but initially it may help to keep a food diary in which you record the food you've eaten as well as any unusual symptoms.

FOR SIZZLING SEX

To inject some sizzle in your sex life, change your routine regularly and be creative. Night-time is not the only time to have sex, nor is the bedroom the only place. See your lover during the day or book yourselves into a favourite hotel, even if it's just for the afternoon!

PROTECT YOUR
VITAL ENERGY

Very hot and very cold drinks
constrict the walls of your arteries,
affecting your blood flow and
'stealing' your vital energy. For good
health, drink liquids that are closer
to room temperature.

A QUICK HEALTH TIP
FOR WOMEN

Drink a glass of water and urinate
after sex to avoid cystitis.

EXERCISE YOUR MEMORY

Did you know that without training
your mind uses approximately one
per cent of its potential? One way to
improve your memory is to start
jotting things down. The act of
writing reinforces your recall
potential, so that you often no
longer need to refer to what you
have written.

TREATING THRUSH

If you're experiencing the discomfort
of vaginal thrush, try mixing one
teaspoon of acidophilus powder with
two or three teaspoons of warm
water. Apply this paste to the
external genital area regularly.

FOR DAMAGED LOCKS

If your hair is lifeless and damaged,
warm two tablespoons of olive oil
over hot water. Massage the oil into
your scalp, then wrap your hair in a
hot towel. When the towel cools,
repeat the process a few times. Wash
your hair thoroughly and rinse it
with a solution made from one part
apple cider vinegar and five parts
warm water.

RUNNING WATER THERAPY

If you can, try to have lunch or
spend some time beside a fountain of
moving water. The negative ions from
the running water are truly
therapeutic and are said to make
people feel happier.

DON'T OVERDO IT

Overuse of medication – particularly
over-the-counter antihistamines,
diuretics and sedatives – can cause
further health problems, fatigue and
a lack of interest in sex. If you feel
you may be overdoing it, see your
doctor or naturopath and discuss
the problem.

PREVENTING STRETCHMARKS

You can prevent stretchmarks from occurring after giving birth if you look after your skin early in your pregnancy. Use apricot kernel oil as a base oil with a few drops of neroli oil, and massage into your skin every evening.

TO HELP YOU UNWIND

To unwind after one of *those* days,
make yourself a cup of organic
chamomile tea (with a pinch of
lavender, if you like) and take the
time to drink it slowly. It relaxes
and settles a nervy stomach.

QUALITY, NOT QUANTITY

Cheap wines often contain high levels
of preservatives and additives that
can upset your stomach and cause an
allergic reaction. Keep an eye out for
high-quality wines. You may pay a
little extra, but you'll be doing your
body a favour.

ANYONE FOR CHESS?

Instead of turning on the television,
play a game with your family or
friends. There are many different
games now available that can involve
a group of people and are really
great fun. And don't forget the
traditional games like chess,
backgammon and cards.

BUCKWHEAT: THE FORGOTTEN GRAIN

Buckwheat is widely eaten in Russia where it's used as a basic energy grain. It helps keep the heart and veins in good health. Cook it like rice for ten minutes, and serve with grated cheese, soy sauce and vegetables.

GET OUT!

Try not to exercise indoors all the time. Consider power walking and enjoy the fresh air, the scenery, the smells, the sounds, the people you pass by.

CONSIDER GREEN TEA

Recent research shows green tea to have extraordinary anti-oxidant properties that help to prevent some forms of cancer. Green tea does contain caffeine, though, so if you have high blood pressure you may want the decaffeinated variety.

CAN'T MAKE
THE DISTANCE?

If you want to enjoy sustained sex
without tiring easily, don't overload
your body with sugar, heavy desserts
and alcohol. This overload disturbs
the sugar levels in your body, which
can cause fatigue.

'DANGER' AND 'OPPORTUNITY'

The Chinese character for 'crisis' is a combination of two words: 'danger' and 'opportunity', so while too much stress can lead to disease, it can also be a great challenge. Try to see the positive potential of your next stressful situation.

TAKE CARE OF YOURSELF

Taking care of yourself is not
self-indulgence: it's survival.
Spend just ten minutes a day
utterly, shamelessly and joyfully
on yourself.